NATIONAL GEOGRAPHIC

MATH BEHIND THE SCIENCE

Crunching Numbers

REBECCA L. JOHNSON

PICTURE CREDITS
Cover: © Superstock. Pages 1, 8 (top), 9 (lower) © Royalty-Free/Corbis; pages 2–3 © George Calef/Masterfile; page 4 (left) © National Optical Astronomy Observatories/Phil Degginger/Color-pic, Inc.; page 4 (right) © Yorgos Nikas/Getty Images; pages 4–5 © Takaji Ochi–V&W/The Image Works; pages 6, 12, 16 Equator Graphics; pages 6–7 © Ed Degginger/Color-pic, Inc.; page 8 (lower) © Bianca Lavies/National Geographic; pages 9 (mid), 20 (right), 20–21 © Hemera Technologies, Inc.; page 9 (top) © Siede Preis/Photodisc; pages 10–11 © Dan Guravich/Photo Researchers; page 11 © Joel Sartore/National Geographic; pages 12–13 © Wayne Barrett/Barrett & MacKay Photo Inc.; page 14 © Dr. Gary Gaugler/Visuals Unlimited; page 15 © David Young-Wolff/Photo Edit; pages 16–17 © Charles Doswell III/Getty Images; page 19 © Tom Stack/Tom Stack & Associates; page 20 (left) © James A. Sugar/Corbis; page 21 © Charles O'Rear/Corbis; pages 22–23 © Mark E. Gibson/Gibson Stock Photography.

E-mail addresses and names are fictitious. Any resemblance to an actual e-mail address or person associated with such address is entirely coincidental.

Produced through the worldwide resources of the National Geographic Society, John M. Fahey, Jr., President and Chief Executive Officer; Gilbert M. Grosvenor, Chairman of the Board; Nina D. Hoffman, Executive Vice President and President, Books and Education Publishing Group.

PREPARED BY NATIONAL GEOGRAPHIC SCHOOL PUBLISHING
Ericka Markman, Senior Vice President and President, Children's Books and Education Publishing Group; Steve Mico, Vice President, Editorial Director; Rosemary Baker, Executive Editor; Barbara Seeber, Editorial Manager; Jim Hiscott, Design Manager; Kristin Hanneman, Illustrations Manager; Matt Wascavage, Manager of Publishing Services; Sean Philpotts, Production Manager.

MANUFACTURING AND QUALITY MANAGEMENT
Christopher A. Liedel, Chief Financial Officer; Phillip L. Schlosser, Director; Clifton M. Brown, Manager.

PROGRAM DEVELOPER
Kate Boehm Jerome

ART DIRECTION
Daniel Banks, Project Design Company

CONSULTANT/REVIEWER
Mary Cavanagh, Math and Science Project Specialist, San Diego County Office of Education

BOOK DEVELOPMENT
Navta Associates

Published by the National Geographic Society
1145 17th Street, N.W.
Washington, D.C. 20036-4688

ISBN-13: 978-0-7922-4592-6
ISBN-10: 0-7922-4592-X

Second Printing May 2012
Printed in Canada

TABLE OF CONTENTS

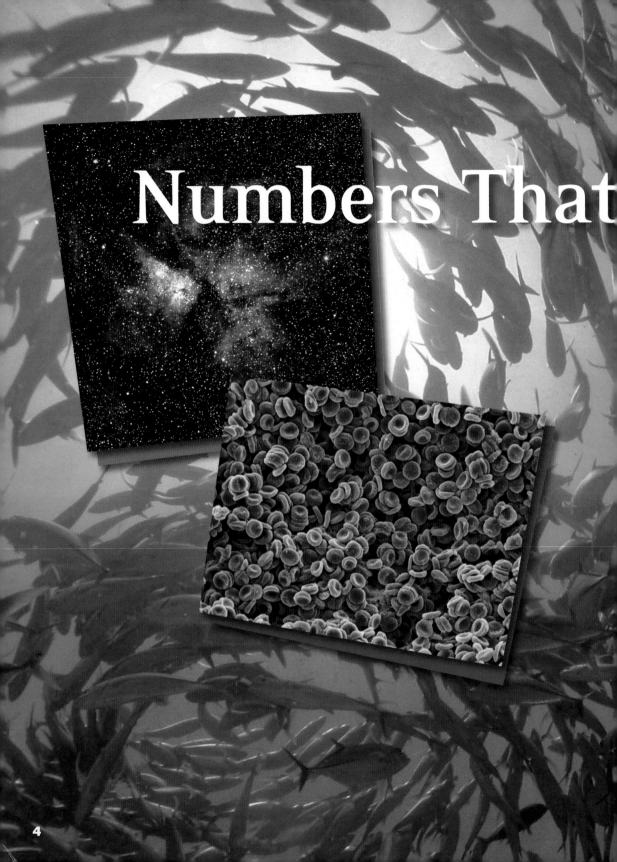

Numbers That

Boggle the Mind

Have you ever looked at the stars and wondered how many are out there in the sky? Astronomers say that there are billions of galaxies. Each galaxy contains billions of stars.

Our lives are full of numbers. Some are easy. How many months are there until your next birthday? Some numbers are so huge they boggle the mind. How many cells are in your body? How many fish are in the ocean?

In science class you'll see a lot of big numbers. But you'll also discover some tricks and tools that make working with those numbers easier. These "number crunchers" range from simple math strategies to the world's most powerful computers. Want some actual experience with number crunching? Several scientists are doing some major number crunching as they e-mail one another from the field. Let's take a look and discover the math behind the science.

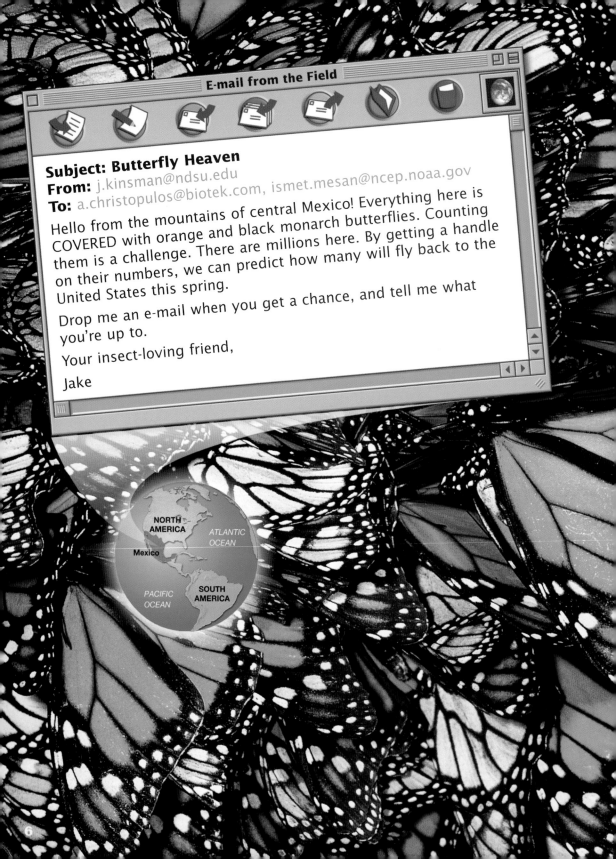

E-mail from the Field

Subject: Butterfly Heaven

From: j.kinsman@ndsu.edu

To: a.christopulos@biotek.com, ismet.mesan@ncep.noaa.gov

Hello from the mountains of central Mexico! Everything here is COVERED with orange and black monarch butterflies. Counting them is a challenge. There are millions here. By getting a handle on their numbers, we can predict how many will fly back to the United States this spring.

Drop me an e-mail when you get a chance, and tell me what you're up to.

Your insect-loving friend,

Jake

NORTH
AMERICA

ATLANTIC
OCEAN

Mexico

PACIFIC
OCEAN

SOUTH
AMERICA

Millions of Monarchs

Y ou've probably seen monarch butterflies in the summertime, flitting from flower to flower. But did you know that monarchs are long-distance travelers?

At the end of summer, millions of monarchs in the United States and Canada head south. They **migrate** thousands of miles to a mountain range in Mexico where they spend the winter. In spring, they fly back north.

Jake is studying this marvelous movement. By counting the butterflies in their wintering grounds, he can figure out how the size of the monarch population changes from year to year. But counting millions of insects takes some serious number crunching.

Around and About

Obviously Jake can't count every monarch. Instead he counts the number of monarchs in a small space. By doing this, he gets a **sample** of the population. Using the sample, he can then estimate how many monarchs there are in a larger area. To **estimate** means to come close to a correct answer. Estimating is an important number-crunching strategy in math.

For example, Jake counts 278 monarchs covering a single tree branch. The tree has 14 similar branches also covered with more monarchs. To estimate the number

of monarchs in the tree, Jake multiplies 278 by 14 to get 3,892.

A Handy Tool

Jake uses a **calculator** to help him multiply quickly as he's counting monarchs. Calculators are one of the simplest number-crunching tools. You can do math quickly with just the touch of a button.

Handy as they are, calculators are no substitute for thinking or learning how to add, subtract, multiply, and divide. These are basic math skills that everyone needs to know. Suppose you used your calculator to multiply 278 by 14 and got 19.86. The powerful "calculator" in your head—your brain—should tell you that the answer isn't right!

Keep It Simple

Jake's estimates are just the beginning. His goal is to figure out about how many monarchs there are per square kilometer. He knows that in this part of the forest, each square kilometer contains about 50 trees.

Jake could multiply 50 trees by 3,892 monarchs per tree to come up with the number of monarchs in one square kilometer. But to make the calculation simpler, he decides to round the number of monarchs per tree. **Rounding** is a type of estimating. It makes big numbers easier to crunch, either in your head or with a tool like a calculator.

Up or Down?

Jake decides he wants to round his estimate of the number of monarchs per tree to the nearest 1,000. The 3 in 3,892 becomes his rounding digit. Next he looks at the number to the right of the 3, which is 8. Since 8 is greater than 5, he rounds up to 4,000.

Now Jake's calculation is easy: $50 \times 4{,}000 = 200{,}000$. So there are about 200,000 monarchs per square kilometer. That's a lot of butterflies!

Estimating and rounding make it easier to work with lots of big numbers. And, if Jake's calculator stops working, doing the calculations with a pencil and some paper will be a breeze!

Rounding Whole Numbers: As Easy as 1, 2, 3!

1. Select the rounding digit (the place value to which you want to round).

2. If the number to the right of the rounding digit is less than 5, change it and all other digits to the right to zeros.

3. If the number to the right of the rounding digit is 5 or greater, first add 1 to the rounding digit, then change all digits to the right of the rounding digit to zeros.

Figuring It Out!

What if Jake's estimate for the number of monarchs per tree had been 3,242 instead of 3,892? Can you follow the steps to round 3,242 to the nearest thousand?

- The rounding digit is still 3.

     3,242

- The number to the right of 3 is now 2.

     3,242

- Since 2 is less than 5, you simply change all the digits to the right of the rounding digit (2, 4, and 2) to zeros.

     3,242 → 3,000

You *rounded down* to 3,000.

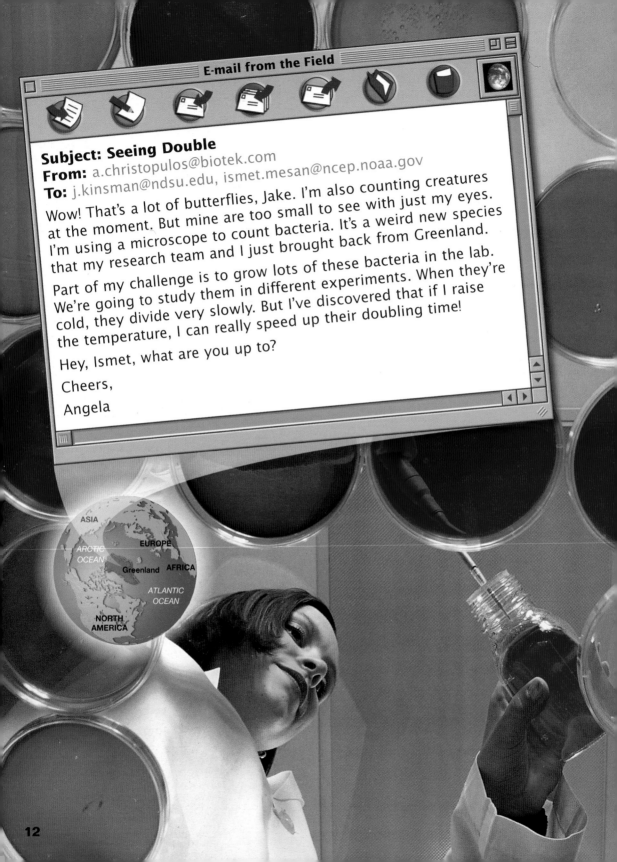

E-mail from the Field

Subject: Seeing Double
From: a.christopulos@biotek.com
To: j.kinsman@ndsu.edu, ismet.mesan@ncep.noaa.gov

Wow! That's a lot of butterflies, Jake. I'm also counting creatures at the moment. But mine are too small to see with just my eyes. I'm using a microscope to count bacteria. It's a weird new species that my research team and I just brought back from Greenland.

Part of my challenge is to grow lots of these bacteria in the lab. We're going to study them in different experiments. When they're cold, they divide very slowly. But I've discovered that if I raise the temperature, I can really speed up their doubling time!

Hey, Ismet, what are you up to?

Cheers,

Angela

ASIA
ARCTIC OCEAN
EUROPE
Greenland AFRICA
ATLANTIC OCEAN
NORTH AMERICA

Simple Cells

Bacteria are some of the simplest forms of life on Earth. Each is just a single cell in size. Bacteria are everywhere. Some live in soil, others in water. There are bacteria on your skin and inside your stomach. A few kinds of bacteria can cause disease. But most are harmless and can even be helpful.

Most bacteria reproduce by splitting in half. Where there was one, suddenly there are two. Those two become four, then eight, and so on. The population doubles every time the bacteria divide.

For her experiments, Angela needs to quickly grow millions of the Greenland bacteria. A number-crunching tool is helping her figure out the best way to complete this task.

Cells of a Different Sort

The tool that Angela is using is a computer **spreadsheet**. You've probably seen paper spreadsheets, like a teacher's grade book or a table that shows the batting averages of baseball players. More complex spreadsheets can be created with computers.

Here's a close look at a bacterium, *Clostridium botulinum* (about 100,000× actual size), that's similar to the one Angela is researching.

A computer spreadsheet is a table of numbers arranged in rows and columns. Each number sits in a box, or **cell**, in the table. Users link each cell to other cells by putting in the mathematical formulas. But you can't see the formulas. The formulas tell the computer to carry out certain calculations. Because the cells in a spreadsheet are linked, if you change a number in one cell, numbers in other cells will change, too.

In her research Angela discovered that the Greenland bacteria divided faster at warmer temperatures. Using this information, Angela came up with a mathematical equation that linked temperature to the time it took the dividing bacteria to reach a population of one million. Then she created a computer spreadsheet that looked like the one below.

Greenland Bacteria Test 1

	A	B	C	D
1		Temperature (in ° Celsius)	Dividing time (in minutes)	Time needed to produce 1 million bacteria (in hours)
2	Trial 1	5	60	20
3	Trial 2	10	42	14
4	Trial 3	15	35	12

What If . . . ?

How is a spreadsheet different from an ordinary table? Because of the equations that link the cells, a spreadsheet is great for answering "*What if . . . ?*" questions. Angela wondered how long it would take to get one million bacteria if they were grown at 13°C. So she changed the number in one cell in the temperature column to 13°C. The spreadsheet instantly did the necessary calculations, and Angela had her answer: 13 hours.

Like calculators, spreadsheets can't think for themselves. Spreadsheets are very powerful tools. But they are only as good as the math that goes into creating them.

	A	B	C	D
		Temperature (in ° Celsius)	Dividing time (in minutes)	Time needed to produce 1 million bacteria (in hours)
1				
2	Trial 1	5	60	20
3	Trial 2	10	42	14
4	Trial 3	13	39.5	13

Greenland Bacteria Test 2

Subject: What's the Weather?
From: ismet.mesan@ncep.noaa.gov
To: a.christopulos@biotek.com, j.kinsman@ndsu.edu

How's the weather in Mexico and Greenland? I'm still a weather nut, and the National Center for Environmental Prediction in Maryland is the perfect place for me. I'm working on computer models used for putting together weather forecasts and warnings all across the United States.

I spend a lot of time sitting in front of a computer monitor. But it's not linked to just any old computer. It's a supercomputer! You should see what it can do and how fast it can do it.

Write soon,

Ismet

NORTH
AMERICA

Maryland

PACIFIC
OCEAN

ATLANTIC
OCEAN

An approaching storm moves its way toward fields in Rosston, Oklahoma.

The Ultimate Number Crunchers

The National Center for Environmental Prediction is a branch of the National Weather Service. It's the starting point for nearly all weather forecasts in the United States.

Forecasts are predictions, or educated estimates, about what's going to happen with the weather in the next hour, day, or week. The forecasts are generated by complex computer programs called computer **models**. Billions of bits of information about temperature, wind, humidity, air pressure, and other factors are fed into these models. These data are processed to become the source for the weather forecasts that you hear on TV or radio.

The Fast Track

Models like those Ismet works with can only run on **supercomputers**. These are the fastest and the most powerful computers in the world. Supercomputers are the ultimate number crunchers.

Imagine 1,000 computers, all connected and working on different parts of a huge problem at the same time. A supercomputer is a bit like that, only better. These powerful number crunchers carry out billions of mathematical calculations every second. Some scientists think that it won't be long before there are supercomputers that can perform trillions of calculations per second!

Supercomputers definitely aren't for doing homework. In addition to weather forecasting, they are used to model how Earth's climate is changing, how new medicines act on body cells, and how air flows around jets traveling hundreds of miles an hour. No other computers are able to tackle problems that involve so much data and have so many different qualities or quantities (**variables**) to compare.

The Human Factor

Supercomputers are good, but they're not perfect. Ismet constantly compares the forecast information her models generate with what she thinks it should be. She frequently makes corrections and improvements in the models.

Maybe someday you'll have the chance to work with the next generation of supercomputers. In the meantime, you've got other technological tools at your fingertips. And don't forget that your brain is still the most marvelous "supercomputer" of all!

Using a wind tunnel, researchers can model the airflow around jets.

Words Count!

Tip

Try to break an unfamiliar word into a root word and a combining form. Once you understand what the two parts mean, the rest is easy.

How big is a kilobyte? How fast is a teraflop? Some of the words used with high-tech number crunching can be mysterious.

But wait! This secret language is simpler than you think.

◀ Try this tip the next time you get stuck.

Prefix	Greek meaning	Computer language meaning
mega-	great	million
giga-	giant	billion
tera-	monstrous	trillion

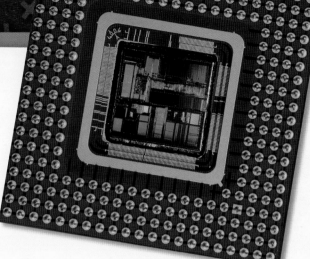

Let's take a closer look at the word *kilobyte*.

1 Identify the root word. Think about what it means.

byte = single unit of information

2 Identify the combining form at the beginning of the word. Think about what it means.

kilo- = one thousand

Kilo- comes from a Greek word that means "one thousand."

3 Put the two word parts together to figure out the meaning.

kilobyte = 1,000 units of computer information

4 Figure out the meanings of other "byte" words. Try *megabyte*, *gigabyte*, and *terabyte*. Use the table to help you.

megabyte = a million bytes

gigabyte = a billion bytes

terabyte = a trillion bytes

Try another one!

Supercomputers deal more with flops than bytes. "Flop" stands for "floating point operations per second." What is a megaflop, gigaflop, and teraflop?

Math Notebook

Fun Facts

- The first scientific pocket calculators were made in 1972.

- Some bacteria can divide every 20 minutes under the right conditions.

- The father of the supercomputer was Seymour Cray. He founded Cray Research, a company that developed the first supercomputer in 1958. The company continued to build the world's fastest supercomputers for many years.

Books to Read

Tang, Greg. *The Grapes of Math*. Scholastic Trade, 2001.

Adler, David A. *Calculator Riddles*. Holiday House, 1995.

Websites to Visit

Discover a "calculator time line" and see pictures of early calculators.
www.vintagecalculators.com

Use an online calculator to figure out how much your weekly allowance would be in Armenian drams or Zambian kwachas.
www.bloomberg.com/analysis/ calculators/currency.html

Check out the current weather forecast.
www.hpc.ncep.noaa.gov/noaa/

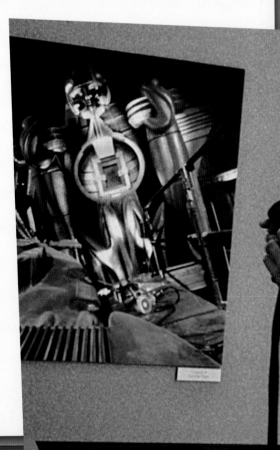

Glossary

bacteria – the simplest forms of life on Earth

calculator – a relatively simple, handheld electronic calculating device

cell – a single box in a spreadsheet

estimate – to come close to a correct answer

forecast – to predict

migrate – to make a special journey from one region to another and then back again at certain times of the year

model – a very complex computer program

rounding – a kind of estimating, where certain digits in large numbers are increased (rounded up) or decreased (rounded down) to make the numbers easier to work with

sample – a part of a population

spreadsheet – a table of cells, organized in rows and columns, that are linked to one another with mathematical formulas

supercomputer – an extremely fast, powerful computer

variable – a quality or quantity that changes

Computers help researchers develop virtual reality technology, which allows users to experience an artificial 3-D environment.

Index